THE CALIFORNIA GOLD RUSH

BY PETER BENOIT

CHILDREN'S PRESS®
An Imprint of Scholastic Inc.
New York Toronto London Auckland Sydney
Mexico City New Delhi Hong Kong
Danbury, Connecticut

BRINGING HISTORY to LIFE

Content Consultant
James Marten, PhD
Professor and Chair, History Department
Marquette University
Milwaukee, Wisconsin

Library of Congress Cataloging-in-Publication Data

Benoit, Peter, 1955–
  The California Gold Rush/by Peter Benoit.
    p. cm.—(Cornerstones of freedom)
  Includes bibliographical references and index.
  ISBN-13: 978-0-531-23053-4 (lib. bdg.)
  ISBN-13: 978-0-531-28153-6 (pbk.)
  1. California—Gold discoveries—Juvenile literature. 2. California—
History—1846-1850—Juvenile literature. 3. Frontier and pioneer life—
California—Juvenile literature. I. Title.
  F865.B47 2012
  979.4′04—dc23   2012000487

5 6 7 8 9 10 R 22 21 20 19 18 17 16

Photographs © 2013: age fotostock: 4 bottom, 8, 40 (Everett Collection
Inc.), 45 (The Print Collector), 19 (Universal Images Group); Alamy Images/
Everett Collection Inc.: back cover; AP Images: 2, 3, 4 top, 7, 10, 12, 14, 16,
42, 44, 46, 51, 56, 57 top, 58, 59 (North Wind Picture Archives), 31, 57 bottom;
Bridgeman Art Library: 6 (Mary Park Seavy Benton/California Historical
Society/Gift of Clara L. Watson), 5 top, 18, 22, 28 (Private Collection/
Peter Newark American Pictures); California State Library/California
History Section: cover; Dreamstime/Bendicks: 5 bottom, 20; iStockphoto/
Duncan Walker: 35; Library of Congress: 48 (Andrew J. Russell), 49 (John
C.H. Grabill); North Wind Picture Archives: 36; Shutterstock, Inc.: 38
(Antonio Abrignani), 55 (Palette7), 32 (ClassicStock.com), 47 (Image Asset
Management Ltd.), 29, 37; The Granger Collection: 26 (George Henry
Burgess), 13 (George Martin Ottinger), 39 (ullstein bild), 11, 21, 23, 27, 41, 54;
The Image Works: 24, 34, 53 foreground (akg-images), 30 (ullstein bild).

Maps by XNR Productions, Inc.

Did you know that studying history can be fun?

BRING HISTORY TO LIFE by becoming a history investigator. Examine the evidence (primary and secondary source materials); cross-examine the people and witnesses. Take a look at what was happening at the time—but be careful! What happened years ago might suddenly become incredibly interesting and change the way you think!

Contents

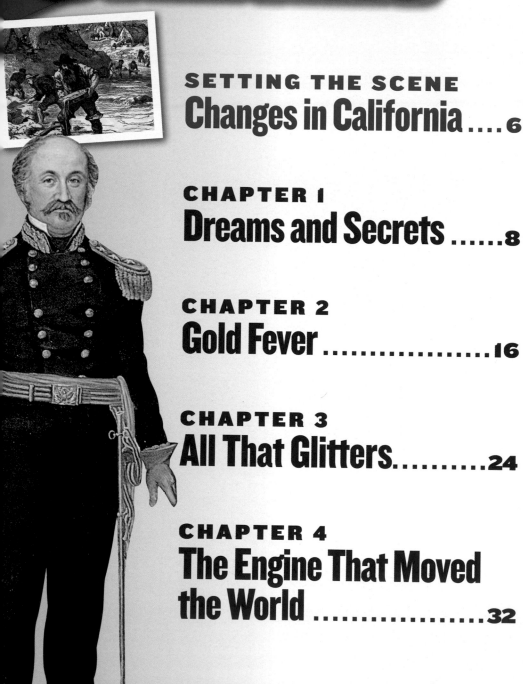

SETTING THE SCENE
Changes in California 6

CHAPTER I
Dreams and Secrets 8

CHAPTER 2
Gold Fever 16

CHAPTER 3
All That Glitters..........24

CHAPTER 4
The Engine That Moved the World 32

CHAPTER 5
Ruined Dreams........... 42

MAP OF THE EVENTS
What Happened Where? 52

THE STORY CONTINUES
American Dreams 54

Influential Individuals 56
Timeline 58
Living History 60
Resources 6 1
Glossary 62
Index.........................63
About the Author.............64

Changes in California

Ranches and farms began being built and developed throughout California in the mid-1800s.

Until February 1848, California was under Mexican control. It was a huge and mostly unsettled area. Earlier Spanish **missions** had largely failed in their efforts to bring Catholicism to the native population. The missions were ended between 1833 and 1840. Mission lands were granted to wealthy people of Spanish descent.

California's economy began to change. Large cattle ranches sprang up on the former mission lands. Native Americans and poor Mexicans worked on these ranches under harsh and dangerous conditions. The pace of change was slow. Trading voyages from the East Coast did not happen often, and only the bravest settlers dared to make the long journey west from their frontier homes.

The discovery of gold at a California sawmill would change this forever. California's population would soon increase rapidly. People from all walks of life traveled there from around the world. Towns and cities appeared almost overnight. Fortunes were made and lost. Some lives were made better. Others were destroyed. The nation as a whole had been set on a new path.

Many settlers moved westward across the United States during the 1800s.

CHAPTER 1

DREAMS and SECRETS

John Sutter settled on land in California that became the first place gold was found in that area.

JOHN SUTTER WAS A MAN

with a dream. He was born in Germany and educated at a military academy in Switzerland. Sutter managed his money poorly and developed a large debt. He would have been imprisoned if he did not pay it, so he fled to America. Sutter never stayed anywhere for very long. He settled briefly in places such as New York, Hawaii, and Alaska. He arrived at last in California's Sacramento Valley in 1839. There, his life would change forever.

New Helvetia, where Sutter's Fort was built, quickly became a bustling center of activity.

New Helvetia

The government granted land to Sutter in June 1841. This land grant fed Sutter's dreams of an **agricultural** paradise. He began by employing hundreds of Native Americans to do the farm's backbreaking labor. Sutter named his settlement New Helvetia after his Swiss homeland. The settlement soon prospered. The native workers dug ditches for **irrigation** and planted crops. They also maintained vineyards and orchards.

Sutter wanted more than just a large farm. He left no stone unturned in his efforts to build a colony. He had established a fort in 1840 to house the workshops and stores that produced the colony's goods. By the middle of the decade, Sutter made plans to build a **gristmill** to grind the wheat that grew on his land. He also planned to grind his neighbors' wheat for profit. He wanted to build a sawmill near pine forests and saw the timber into boards for his construction plans. But Sutter lacked the skills to complete these plans. That was until James Marshall and a group of Mormons, religious followers of *The Book of Mormon*, arrived at the fort.

Sutter's Fort

Sutter's Fort was established in 1840 in what is Sacramento, California, today. It was the business center of Sutter's agricultural empire. Its walls were 2.5 feet (0.76 meters) thick and nearly 18 feet (5.5 m) high. Sutter lived in a brick building at the fort's center. Important buildings lined the fort's four sides. They included a bakery, a granary, and a flour mill. The fort also had shops for carpenters, blacksmiths, and wagon repairs. It had a saloon and kitchen. It was later overrun by gold seekers and destroyed, but it has since been fully restored.

James Marshall

James W. Marshall was born and raised in New Jersey. He traveled west from New Jersey to Kansas and from Kansas to Oregon. He eventually arrived at Sutter's Fort in July 1845. Sutter was impressed by Marshall's skills as a craftsman. He offered Marshall work and helped him purchase land for his own ranch.

Mexico went to war with the United States the next year. Marshall sided with the United States and joined the military. He saw very little combat and returned to his ranch after leaving the military in 1847. There, he found that his cattle had been stolen. Without cattle, Marshall ran into money trouble and lost his ranch. He went back to Sutter's Fort looking for work. Sutter told him about his idea for the sawmill. Marshall agreed to begin scouting for a location along the nearby American River. He soon found a suitable place to build the mill.

Sutter's luck seemed to be improving. A Mormon **battalion** that had also served in the war found its way to Sutter's Fort after leaving the military. The soldiers planned to purchase supplies and then go east to the

James Marshall agreed to run Sutter's Mill in exchange for a share of the wood it produced.

The Mormon battalion was the only U.S. military unit ever to be organized based on religion.

Great Salt Lake in what is now Utah to reconnect with their community. But harsh weather made the journey too difficult. They turned back to the fort and soon found work with Marshall building the foundation for Sutter's sawmill.

A FIRSTHAND LOOK AT
SUTTER'S LETTER

John Sutter wrote to the *San Francisco Pacific News* on October 9, 1849. The letter describes Sutter's shock as Marshall first showed him the glittering gold he had found near the mill. See page 60 for a link to see the letter online.

The site of Sutter's Mill is now a California state historic park.

Gold!

The work was exhausting. The men were not used to such hard labor. Many fell ill, delaying the project. Autumn rains and snow began unusually early in 1847, also causing delays. Marshall knew that the Mormon workers would leave once spring arrived. The project seemed unlikely to ever be completed.

Despite these setbacks, Marshall continued working on the mill. He knew that the mill could operate properly only if the water flowed into it a certain way. That would require careful work. On the morning of January 24, 1848,

Marshall walked along the construction site to make sure everything was going according to plan. He saw a few bright sparkles in a shallow pool of water near the mill. Curious, Marshall scooped up the pea-size pieces of material and took a closer look. He quickly returned to where the men had begun working and announced that he had found gold. The men did not believe him at first. But they soon realized Marshall was telling the truth.

A VIEW FROM ABROAD

Australians watched the developments in California with great interest. An Australian man named E. H. Hargraves traveled to California and saw the gold rush firsthand. He also noticed the area's similarities to New South Wales in Australia. He returned home and used what he had learned to predict where in Australia he might find gold. He was right! By 1851, an Australian gold rush was in full swing. Hundreds of thousands of people traveled to Australia from countries such as China and the United Kingdom.

Marshall made his way back to the fort and told Sutter what he had found. Sutter's carefully laid plans for an agricultural empire seemed to unravel before his eyes. He knew that treasure seekers would overrun the area if word of the gold discovery got out. Sutter and Marshall agreed that it was in their best interest to tell no one what Marshall had found.

CHAPTER 2

GOLD FEVER

Sam Brannan was one of the first people to spread the word about gold being found at Sutter's Mill.

MARSHALL'S DISCOVERY

would not remain a secret for long. A man named
Sam Brannan quickly realized that people were
using gold for purchases. Brannan was a Maine-
born businessman and journalist. He had traveled
as part of a group of more than 200 Mormons
from New York to San Francisco by boat. They
landed at the end of July 1846. Brannan began
a newspaper called the *California Star* soon after
arriving. He also opened a general store at Sutter's
Fort. There, he eventually encountered some of
Sutter's Mormon workers. They paid for goods
from Brannan's store with gold.

Some of the typical tools that gold seekers used for mining were pickaxes, pans, shovels, and rakes.

Brannan's Plan

Brannan got an idea about how to profit from the workers. He set about purchasing every shovel, pan, and pickax in California so he could resell them. He thought that he could make at least as much money supplying gold seekers as he could panning for gold himself.

He drummed up business by walking through the streets of San Francisco shouting, "Gold! Gold! Gold from the American River!" Not everyone believed him. Many had heard tales about gold from the Sacramento Valley. But the sight of the gold that people had found provided proof. Soon, word spread to the nearby towns of Monterey and Los Angeles, and then beyond. **Prospectors** stopped at Brannan's store to purchase mining supplies. Brannan would eventually become California's first millionaire.

Brannan had given California gold fever. But Lieutenant William Tecumseh Sherman would soon spread it to the rest of the country. The Treaty of Guadalupe Hidalgo ended the Mexican-American War and made California part of the United States in 1848. Sherman and California military governor R. B. Mason arrived at Sutter's Mill to gather information about reported gold discoveries. Mason saw firsthand

Lieutenant William Tecumseh Sherman helped bring news of the gold discovery to the eastern part of the country.

Prospectors discovered gold in the form of dust, flakes, and larger chunks.

evidence of vast amounts of gold. He knew officials in Washington, D.C., would want proof of the gold discovery. He purchased gold dust and sent it back East, where it arrived months later. On August 19, the *New York Herald* became the first eastern newspaper to report on Sutter's gold.

A FIRSTHAND LOOK AT
MASON'S OFFICIAL REPORT ON THE GOLD MINES

R. B. Mason issued a lengthy report to his superiors in Washington, D.C. It detailed the mining operations that had already begun and the amount of money made by Sam Brannan's general store. Mason's report described California as a land of incredible riches. See page 60 for a link to view it online.

Finally, President James K. Polk confirmed the discovery in an address to Congress on December 5, 1848. Sutter's gold was a secret no more.

By Land or by Sea

The earliest gold seekers came from places near the Sacramento Valley. They used simple mining tools such as pans and long toms to collect large amounts of gold with little effort. Some of these early prospectors found thousands of dollars worth of the precious metal in a single day. News of successes encouraged more people to join the hunt for gold.

Gold seekers from the East Coast rarely chose a land route to California. Instead, they sailed more than 12,000 miles (19,312 kilometers) around South America's Cape Horn. The voyage usually took six

SPOTLIGHT ON

Long Toms

The long tom was a trough about 12 to 15 feet (3.6 to 4.6 m) long and 2 feet (0.6 m) wide. It was made of wood and a metal bottom. One end had a screen that allowed water to flow out. Long toms were used to find gold in river sand, mud, and gravel. One or more people shoveled dirt and sand into the trough. Others mixed in water and removed larger stones that could damage the device. Long toms allowed for mining on a much larger scale than pan mining did. However, they required teams of six to eight people to work together.

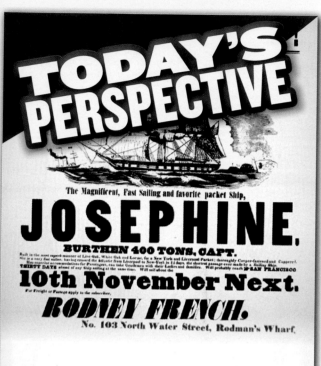

The Magnificent, Fast Sailing and favorite packet Ship,

JOSEPHINE,

BURTHEN 400 TONS, CAPT.

10th November Next.

RODNEY FRENCH,

No. 103 North Water Street, Rodman's Wharf,

Posters advertising the voyage around Cape Horn painted a rosy picture of the long journey. Many companies claimed that their ships were among the fastest. Others suggested that passengers would share in the company's profits from trade or mining. Many of these promises turned out to be false. Many gold seekers and other people did not want to travel by land because they were worried about attacks by Native Americans. They thought traveling by sea would be safer. We now know that native groups rarely attacked settlers. Disease, both on the ships and on overland routes, claimed many more lives.

months or longer. Passengers endured rough journeys. Their ships pressed on through horrific storms, and some of them sank. Water stored for the passengers often became undrinkable. Their food was infested with insects. There were no fresh fruits or vegetables. Rats living on the ships brought disease and death.

The journey over land was more direct and less expensive. This made it the only option for some gold seekers. Most followed the 2,000 miles (3,219 km) of the California Trail, which stretched from towns on the Missouri River to Fort Hall, Idaho. It then turned southwest to cross the Sierra Nevada and turned toward the goldfields on the American River. Settlers often encountered Native Americans on the journey. Many of the settlers were eager to trade or sell supplies. The Native Americans rarely attacked unless they were provoked. But the settlers faced other difficulties. Diseases such as typhoid, malaria, and cholera took many lives.

Many of the land travelers were unprepared for the hardships of the wilderness. They expected the journey to be a grand adventure. They often found danger instead. Reaching the goldfields of California was a struggle. Once there, gold seekers often assumed they would reap fortune quickly and return home wealthy. But this would not be the case for most of them.

The journey west was long and difficult, and many people did not survive the trip.

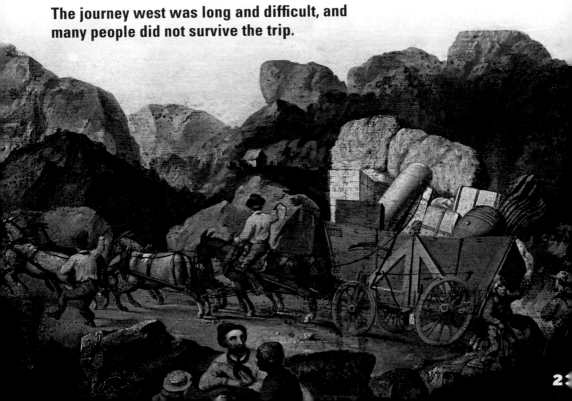

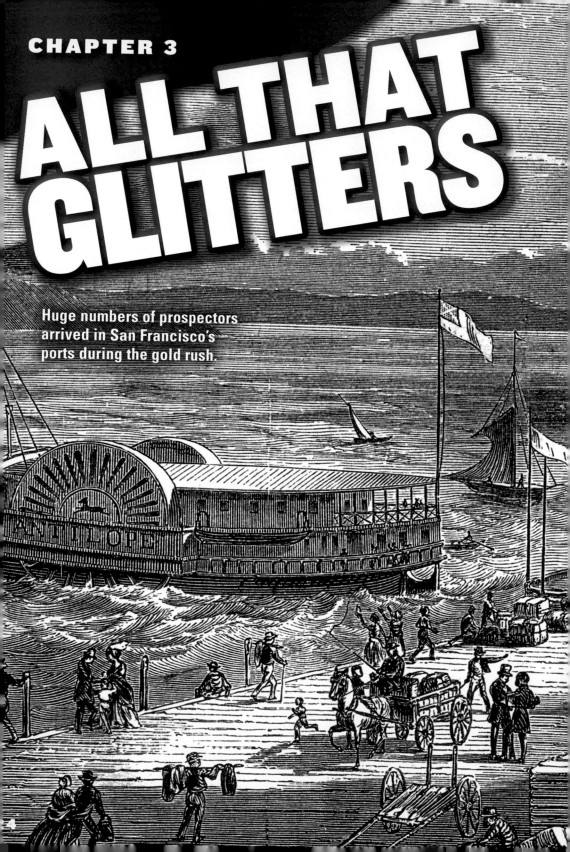

CHAPTER 3

ALL THAT GLITTERS

Huge numbers of prospectors arrived in San Francisco's ports during the gold rush.

NOTHING COULD HAVE

prepared the treasure seekers for what they would find. Sea travelers found it difficult just to go ashore in San Francisco. When ships arrived, the crews abandoned them and hurried to the American River to seek their fortunes. Once travelers arrived on land, they were given no established rules for land use. Anyone could stake a claim to California's lands. This meant that the first to arrive stood the greatest chance of success. Opportunities could appear and disappear almost immediately. This made California a bustling center of activity during the early days of the gold rush.

Small mining towns sprang up across California during the gold rush.

Dust in the Wind

The first buildings constructed by gold seekers were little more than canvas stretched over whatever boards the miners found. Towns appeared almost instantly wherever gold was discovered. Some of the towns survived as supply centers or more permanent settlements. But many towns vanished once prospectors had exhausted the area's easily obtained gold. Some settlements had names reflecting the ethnicity of their inhabitants. Chinese miners were excluded from the largely white-populated Camp Salvado when they arrived in 1849. As a result, they started their own settlement called Chinese Camp. At its peak, the town was home to 5,000 Chinese miners.

Daily life was much the same everywhere. San Francisco was a small settlement of perhaps 1,000 people in 1848. It was deserted in the first weeks and months of the gold rush as its inhabitants rushed east in search of gold. However, San Francisco would not remain deserted for long.

Gold seekers continued to stream into the Sacramento Valley through San Francisco in huge numbers. Some people realized that providing goods and services for miners would be a sure

YESTERDAY'S HEADLINES

Some of the best writing about life during the California gold rush was by Dame Shirley. Dame Shirley was the pen name of Louise Clapp. Clapp spent more than a year with her husband, a doctor, at two mining camps on the Feather River. Her colorful descriptions appeared regularly in the magazine the *Pioneer*. They were at times alarming. Mining town housing was crude, and bars were everywhere. Temptation was constant. Clapp's writing describes how some miners lost everything they had as a result of bad decisions.

Women were a rare sight in the early days of the gold rush.

source of income. The miners needed tools to find gold.
They also needed clothes, food, and shelter. Saloons
would give the miners a place to relax after working hard
all day.

A New American Dream

Farms, stores, and churches—and the people to build
them—were all needed to service the miners. Schools and
hotels were built as women and children began to move

to California in greater numbers. By the end of 1849, the population of San Francisco had grown to more than 20,000. The city changed continuously. Dozens of new buildings were completed each week.

New arrivals to San Francisco wrote to their families and friends. They described the wonders of great wealth and opportunity they witnessed. They also wrote of the city's troubles. Gambling, alcohol, and murder were common in the mining settlements. The miners spent

San Francisco grew larger as more and more gold prospectors arrived in California.

their newly made money without thinking. The secure, orderly lives many had left behind a few months before were forgotten in this new land.

Many prospectors lost the gold they had found by gambling on card games.

Between 1849 and 1851, six major fires occurred in San Francisco, destroying many buildings. Each time it was rebuilt, the city became grander, more bustling, and more **cosmopolitan**. But it still suffered from the same problems of crime and filthy, unhealthy conditions. It seemed like chaos to the many miners who were not used to life in a large city.

The successes of men such as Sam Brannan and store owner Levi Strauss stirred up excitement and adventure in California. Many people who traveled there in those early years felt they were free to fail. They did not worry what friends and family might think of them. They took chances they would never have taken otherwise. This spirit of adventure carried the nation forward into a new era.

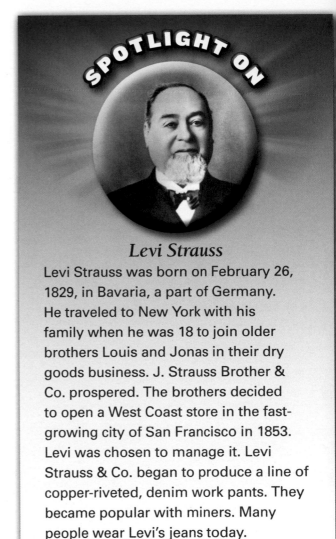

SPOTLIGHT ON

Levi Strauss

Levi Strauss was born on February 26, 1829, in Bavaria, a part of Germany. He traveled to New York with his family when he was 18 to join older brothers Louis and Jonas in their dry goods business. J. Strauss Brother & Co. prospered. The brothers decided to open a West Coast store in the fast-growing city of San Francisco in 1853. Levi was chosen to manage it. Levi Strauss & Co. began to produce a line of copper-riveted, denim work pants. They became popular with miners. Many people wear Levi's jeans today.

CHAPTER 4

The ENGINE THAT MOVED THE WORLD

New railroads made it easier to travel and ship goods across the country.

THE GOLD RUSH DID NOT ONLY transform California. It also had a major effect throughout the world. The newly discovered gold stimulated economies around the globe. It also caused a revolution in transportation and turned California into an agricultural powerhouse. New roads and railways were built. Countless churches and schools were constructed throughout the West. The great movement westward prompted by the gold rush reshaped the United States forever.

Many new buildings were constructed as San Francisco continued to grow.

Onward and Upward

The changes that occurred in California were major. The migration to the goldfields of the Sacramento Valley swelled the population statewide. San Francisco's growth was particularly dramatic. In 1847, it was a small Mexican port with a population of 500. By 1870, the city's population had surged past 150,000. San Francisco had become a major center of national and international activity.

Population growth caused a rapid expansion of agriculture in the region. At first, farms provided food for California's miners and **entrepreneurs**. California's transportation links to the world were limited, so it was impractical to export the state's agricultural products. For the same reason, imports were also limited. But gold created jobs and stimulated investment in manufacturing and agriculture. Miners and businesspeople returning to Chile, China, Australia, and Europe brought gold and wondrous stories of a land of boundless potential. Soon, goods from China, Great Britain, and Australia began arriving in San Francisco.

Ships carrying goods from all around the world began coming into San Francisco's ports during the gold rush.

Pacific Mail's transportation system made it easy for prospectors to ship their gold around the world.

Gold also funded transportation projects large and small. Many local roads were built in California. But some investors realized that California's potential could only be fully realized if a network of railroads and steamships supported it.

One of the most successful transportation companies was the Pacific Mail Steamship Company. It was started in April 1848 by a group of New York City merchants led by William Henry Aspinwall. The company originally planned to transport agricultural products grown by

John Sutter and others. But it soon enlarged its interests to include gold from the American River. The company also provided regular transportation of miners, entrepreneurs, and **speculators**. It was an important part of San Francisco's growth. It began regular steamship service connecting San Francisco with Hong Kong and Japan in 1867.

Pacific Mail recognized that transporting gold

The Panama Railroad

William Henry Aspinwall was the driving force behind the formation of the Pacific Mail Steamship Company. In 1850, he was faced with the difficult task of building a railroad over the Isthmus of Panama. His workers encountered countless obstacles. Costs soon soared well above the project's original budget. The Panama Railroad was finally completed in 1855, five years after construction began.

efficiently would increase the company's wealth and power. It pushed to build a railway across the Isthmus of Panama. California gold was carried by steamship down the coast to Panama. It was then carried overland by rail, and finally by steamship to cities on the East Coast. One of the steamships was named the SS *Central America*. In September 1857, it sank 160 miles (257 km) off the North Carolina coast in a hurricane. Three tons of gold settled on the bottom of the Atlantic Ocean.

The sinking of the SS *Central America* in September 1857 caused a great deal of debate. One of the ship's surviving officers protested when some people claimed that the ship had not been seaworthy. He believed that it had been capable of withstanding any storm. He claimed that the ship boilers failed because of a "lack of a proper supply of coal." Historians now believe that a seal on one of the paddle wheels ruptured and let water flow in. The boiler began to fail. This caused the failure of the pumps and the paddle wheels needed to steer the *Central America*.

Order out of Chaos

After the Mexican-American War ended and the Treaty of Guadalupe Hidalgo was signed in 1848, the task of creating a constitution for California was begun. Many people discussed holding a constitutional convention, an official meeting of representatives to write a constitution. They also wanted California to become a U.S. state. Brigadier General Bennet Riley, California's military governor, gave this movement form and direction. He proposed that 37 delegates be drawn from every part of California. The delegates were elected on August 1, 1849.

One month later, the number of delegates had grown to 48. Many delegates were lawyers, ranchers, or merchants. Others were bankers, surveyors, printers, doctors, or soldiers. Less than one-third of the delegates had been in California longer than three years. Many came from the East or Midwest. Others came from Scotland, Spain, or France. California's first constitution was completed and signed in just a few weeks. The delegates **ratified** it on November 13, 1849. They then traveled to Washington, D.C., to seek statehood.

The U.S. victory in the Mexican-American War led to California's annexation and ultimately its statehood.

A FIRSTHAND LOOK AT
THE CONSTITUTION OF THE STATE OF CALIFORNIA

California's constitution was created and ratified during the height of the gold rush. It helped pave the way for California to gain statehood. See page 60 for a link to view the constitution's original text online.

California became a state the following year as part of the Compromise of 1850. The compromise was created during a heated debate over slavery in the United States. The compromise controlled the spread of slavery

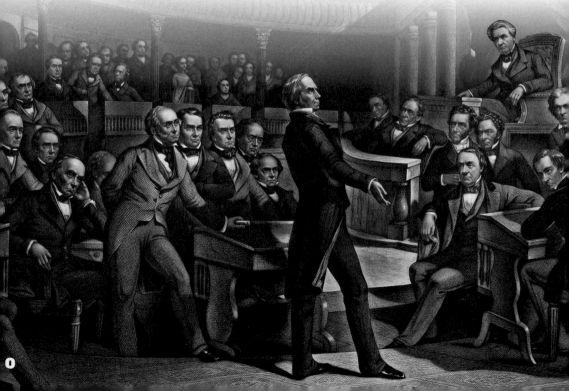

Senator Henry Clay of Kentucky proposed the Compromise of 1850 in a speech before his fellow senators.

Some prospectors used enslaved workers to help look for gold.

by creating a balance between the number of states that allowed slavery and those that did not. The 48 delegates at California's constitutional convention had all rejected slavery. Slave states such as South Carolina, Mississippi, Georgia, and Alabama did not want to allow California into the Union. Differences over slavery would eventually be a major cause of the Civil War.

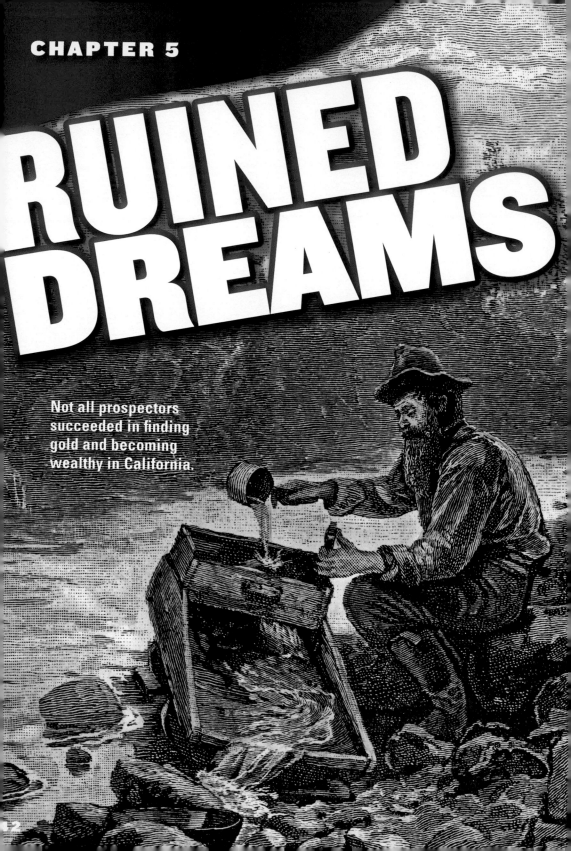

CHAPTER 5

RUINED DREAMS

Not all prospectors succeeded in finding gold and becoming wealthy in California.

THE UNITED STATES WAS

affected by the gold rush in many different ways. Some changes were for the better and some for the worse. The shining metal lying in the pool near John Sutter's sawmill two years earlier had brought great promise to California. In fact, it had reshaped the entire nation. But the gold rush had ruined John Sutter's dreams. Gold seekers had destroyed his fort. His agricultural empire was trampled and forgotten. The gold rush also left countless miners financially ruined or even dead.

Gold prospecting was easy for almost anyone to do, partly because it required only simple, available equipment.

Sorting Things Out

Success was easier for gold miners to achieve in 1848 and 1849 than in later years. At that time, gold was plentiful and lay close to the surface. Often, all that was required was patience, a willingness to work long hours, and a large metal pan. Miners needed only to shake the pan from side to side to slosh sand, gravel, and excess water away. This left the heavier gold in the bottom of the pan. It did not require specialized equipment or cooperation with other miners. All of that would change. As gold became more difficult to obtain, gold mining required processing larger amounts of sand and dirt, which meant miners would have to work together.

Ethnic hatred was a way of life in many settlements. The international scope of California's gold rush threw together people who had nothing in common except a desire for instant wealth. American miners bristled at competition from Asia, Europe, and South America. Miners who spoke different languages or had different customs were mistrusted. Chileans and Mexicans were singled out and persecuted. Some Americans blamed all of California's problems on foreign miners. In 1852, the Foreign Miner's Tax required all foreign miners to purchase mining licenses at great expense.

Mexican and Latin American miners often brought workers, who were paid very little, to assist them. In

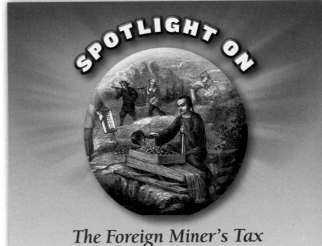

SPOTLIGHT ON

The Foreign Miner's Tax

In 1852, Chinese miners were ineligible for U.S. citizenship. There were more than 25,000 Chinese miners working in the Sacramento Valley, making them the largest foreign group there. The Foreign Miner's Tax placed heavy demands on Chinese miners to generate tax revenues. The tax often amounted to half of a miner's monthly income! To make matters worse, the state court decision *People v. Hall* (1854) made it impossible for Chinese people to testify against white Americans in court. The tax and the new law gave white miners great power to keep their Chinese rivals out of the goldfields.

addition, Mexicans often had considerable knowledge about mining. Both of these things allowed them to compete well against American miners. Some southern slaveholders brought enslaved people to mine gold. Many other miners were unhappy with this. Most of them did not disagree with the idea of slavery. Instead, they were upset that working beside slaves made them seem like little more than slaves themselves.

The frustrations that had previously been bearable erupted in violent actions as prices rose and gold became harder to find. Murder became common. Ordinary miners were faced with the knowledge that they were being displaced and defeated.

Sudden violence was common in mining camps.

Eventually, only mining companies could manage the expense of removing the remaining gold. More efficient mining techniques were developed. **Hydraulic mining** diverted water at higher elevations into wooden **flumes**. The force of gravity caused the water to speed up. It exploded from nozzles with an awesome force. The blast of water tore huge amounts of gravel from mountainsides. The mix of gravel, gold, and water passed through huge **sluices**. Gold was deposited in the sluices. The gravel was then dumped into creeks and river canyons.

This destroyed many ecosystems. The

TODAY'S PERSPECTIVE

By 1853, deposits along rivers and streams were already producing less gold. The long tom was no longer enough for finding significant amounts of gold. That year, Edward Matteson pioneered hydraulic mining in California. Immense sluices were built, and water was fired at an amazing speed, washing away entire hillsides. The amount of sediment moved was enormous, but farmlands were destroyed. Rivers and streams clogged with sediment. Hydraulic mining was considered a brilliant innovation over 150 years ago. But today, it is easy to see the negative side of hydraulic mining and the thoughtless destruction it caused.

Hydraulic mining caused many environmental problems.

water flooded farmlands downstream. It often buried
crops under thick layers of gravel. Farmers complained
bitterly. But gold mines generated large tax revenues.
For this reason, legislators did not want to rule against
miners. Rivers gradually became clogged with sediment
and then impassable as hydraulic mining continued.
Finally, in 1884, Judge Lorenzo Sawyer ruled against
the mining companies by making hydraulic mining
illegal. The ruling saved the remainder of the region's
farmlands.

Tension with Native Americans

The combination of hydraulic mining and the huge
number of miners degraded California's ecosystems and
wildlife habitats. Waste-polluted rivers and forestlands
were cleared to make room for settlements. California's
Native Americans saw their hunting grounds disappear,
taken over by the miners for their own purposes. Rivers
where salmon swam were polluted. Hungry miners
thinned out the deer population. Native Americans
began starving because of the lack of wild game, so they
raided mining camps. Miners retaliated by killing Native

**Hydraulic miners had little regard for
the rights of the Native Americans
whose land they destroyed.**

Americans. Tensions between the two groups rose during the winter months, when Native Americans' needs were greatest and the miners had more time to launch attacks.

Native Americans working in the mines were often treated harshly. Many were driven out of camp or murdered. The Native American population soon began to plummet. Attacks, diseases, kidnapping, and starvation decreased the native population by more than 80 percent. Families were torn apart. Entire cultures were destroyed.

California's **legislature** gave its support to ethnic hatred by passing the Act for the Government and Protection of Indians in 1850. Any Native Americans lingering near a mining camp could potentially be indentured. This meant they would be forced to work in mines, but receive no wages. They would be given only a small amount of food and clothing. Miners exploited the law for their own purposes. They raided native villages and kidnapped people. Native Americans not needed in the mines were sold to farmers and ranchers as slaves.

A FIRSTHAND LOOK AT
THE ACT FOR THE GOVERNMENT AND PROTECTION OF INDIANS

This California act of 1850 allowed white settlers to force Native Americans to work for them. It also denied Native Americans freedoms that citizens today routinely take for granted. It contributed to the destruction of California's native groups. See page 60 for a link to read the act online.

The California gold rush was a major event in the history and transformation of the United States.

The California gold rush stands as a remarkable example of the power of hope, imagination, and hard work. It transformed the world, but at the cost of many lives and the environment. Ethnic hatred and greed were unfortunate results of the gold rush, and should not be forgotten in light of the positive developments that also occurred.

What Happened Where?

Sutter's Mill

Sutter's Fort

South Fork American River

San Francisco

●Chinese Camp

CALIFORNIA

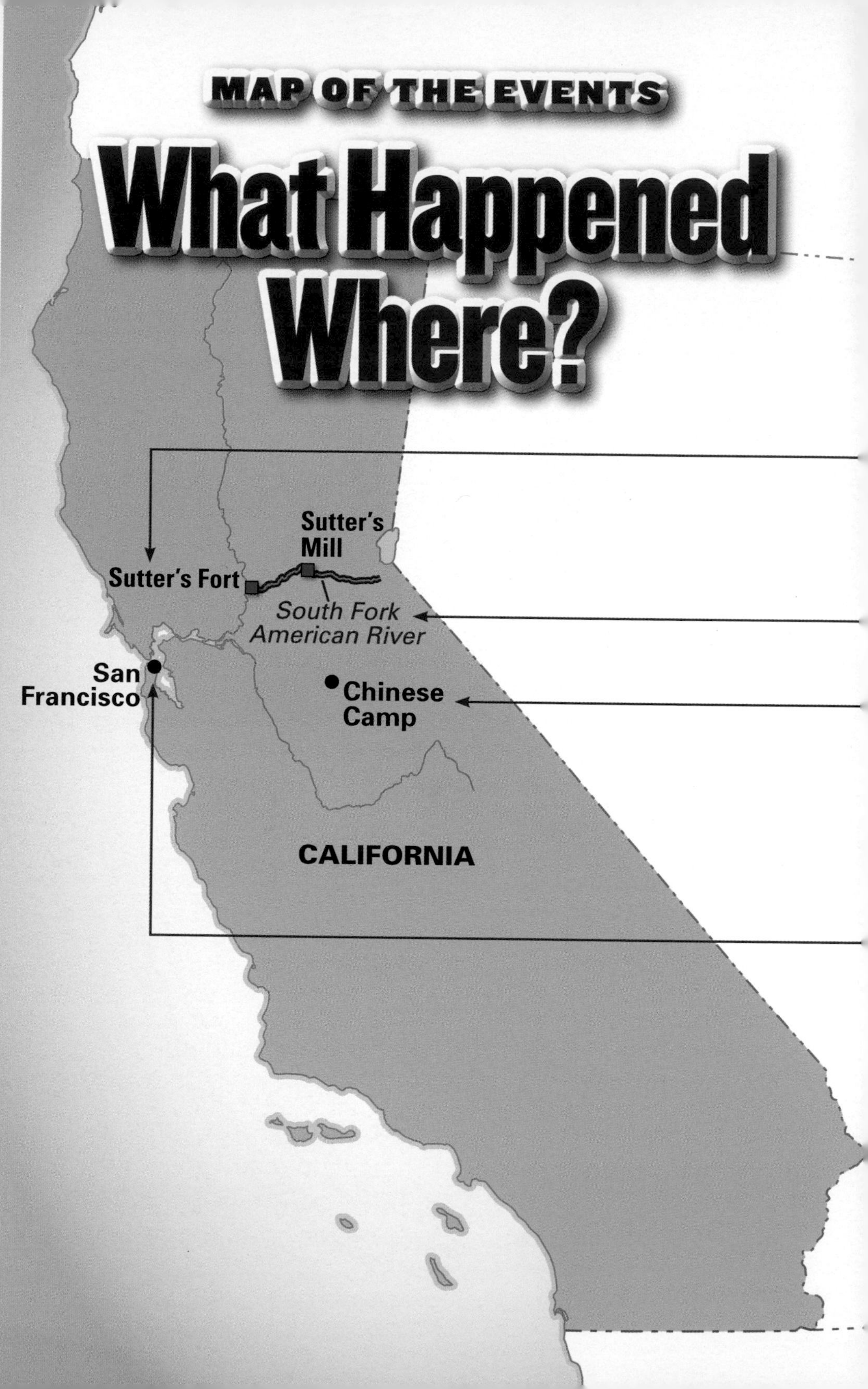

Sutter's Fort John Sutter originally planned to build an agricultural empire, but his dreams were shattered when gold was discovered on his land in 1848.

American River Thousands of miners panned for gold along this river during the gold rush.

Chinese Camp Chinese miners formed their own settlement when they were rejected from Camp Salvado in 1849. Some 5,000 Chinese gold miners lived and worked at the camp during the height of the gold rush.

 **San Francisco** In just a few short years, the gold rush transformed San Francisco from a small port into a major city as tens of thousands of people traveled there in search of fortune.

N
W E
S

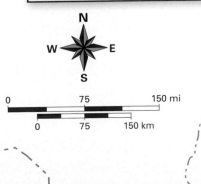

0   75   150 mi

0   75   150 km

American Dreams

Many businesspeople grew wealthy in San Francisco during the gold rush.

The California gold rush was in many ways a turning point in American history. It helped bring about a rapid expansion of industry and transportation. It also drew Americans westward seeking a better life.

BY 2011, MORE THAN 800,000

It created wealth for merchants and entrepreneurs as well as miners. It also brought hope for a life with more opportunities and a greater amount of self-determination. The American Dream and its "pursuit of happiness" had previously been tied to the morals and practices of **Puritanism**. Afterward, it would be identified with wealth and personal independence.

The desire for wealth and freedom continues to influence and motivate many Americans to this day. We still struggle with how best to balance material success with cultural sensitivity and environmental responsibility. If the great journey taken by thousands of gold seekers in 1849 has taught us anything, it is how far we still have to go.

San Francisco has grown to become one of the largest cities in the United States.

PEOPLE WERE LIVING IN SAN FRANCISCO.

INFLUENTIAL INDIVIDUALS

James K. Polk (1795–1849) was the 11th president of the United States. His announcement to Congress about the gold discovery in California accelerated the gold rush in December 1848.

John Sutter (1803–1880) was one of the most influential men in California before the gold rush. The gold rush began when gold was found in a shallow pool near Sutter's sawmill.

James Marshall

William Henry Aspinwall (1807–1875) was a New York City businessman who was one of the founders of the Pacific Mail Steamship Company. He also helped build the Panama Railroad, which made it easier to transport gold around the world.

James Marshall (1810–1885) partnered with John Sutter to help Sutter expand his agricultural empire. Marshall was foreman of the crew building Sutter's sawmill. He discovered the gold that would capture the world's imagination.

Sam Brannan (1819–1889) was a businessman and a journalist. He told the secret of Sutter's gold discovery, setting off the scramble for gold.

William Tecumseh Sherman (1820–1891) was an American military officer who helped oversee California at the end of the Mexican-American War. He sent a large sample of gold to Washington, D.C., to convince President James K. Polk of California's riches.

Levi Strauss (1829–1902) began a dry goods business in San Francisco in 1853. In 1873, he began manufacturing the denim work pants that made him famous.

Sam Brannan

Levi Strauss

TIMELINE

1840

John Sutter begins building Sutter's Fort and requests a land grant, which he receives a year later.

1845

July
James Marshall meets Sutter.

1846

July
Sam Brannan arrives in San Francisco.

1847

Autumn
Work begins on Sutter's sawmill.

1849

Chinese miners arrive in California.

November 13
California's constitution is ratified.

December
San Francisco's population is more than 20,000.

1850

California is added to the Union as a free state; the Act for the Government and Protection of Indians passes.

1853

Levi Strauss opens a dry goods store in San Francisco.

1848

1848–1850

January 24
Marshall discovers gold near Sutter's sawmill.

February 2
The Treaty of Guadalupe Hidalgo is signed.

April
The Pacific Mail Steamship Company is formed.

May 12
Brannan announces Sutter's gold discovery in San Francisco.

August 19
The *New York Herald* reports on California gold.

December 5
President James K. Polk mentions California gold while addressing Congress.

The first wave of gold miners arrives in California.

1857

1870

1884

September
The SS *Central America* sinks in a hurricane off the North Carolina coast.

San Francisco's population is more than 150,000.

Judge Lorenzo Sawyer's ruling ends hydraulic mining in California's goldfields.

LIVING HISTORY

Primary sources provide firsthand evidence about a topic. Witnesses to a historical event create primary sources. They include autobiographies, newspaper reports of the time, oral histories, photographs, and memoirs. A secondary source analyzes primary sources, and is one step or more removed from the event. Secondary sources include textbooks, encyclopedias, and commentaries. To view the following primary and secondary sources, go to www.factsfornow.scholastic.com. Enter the keywords **Gold Rush** and look for the Living History logo Σ¡.

Σ¡ The Act for the Government and Protection of Indians

This 1850 act placed unfair restrictions on Native Americans and made it illegal for them to testify against whites in court.

Σ¡ The Constitution of the State of California, 1849

California's state constitution was created at the peak of the gold rush. Its creators hoped to gain statehood for the rapidly growing region.

Σ¡ Mason's Official Report on the Gold Mines

California military governor R. B. Mason prepared an official report detailing his and Lieutenant William Tecumseh Sherman's visit to Sutter's Mill.

Σ¡ Sutter's Letter

John Sutter's letter to the *San Francisco Pacific News* describes his reactions to the discovery of gold on his land.

Σ¡ The Writings of Reverend Albert Williams

The Reverend Albert Williams wrote of the fires and other troubles he witnessed in San Francisco.

RESOURCES

Books

Brown, Don. *Gold! Gold from the American River!* New York: Roaring Brook Press, 2011.

Olson, Tod. *How to Get Rich in the California Gold Rush: An Adventurer's Guide to the Fabulous Riches Discovered in 1848.* Washington, DC: National Geographic, 2008.

Somervill, Barbara A. *The Gold Rush: Buried Treasure.* New York: Children's Press, 2005.

Visit this Scholastic Web site for more information on the California Gold Rush:
www.factsfornow.scholastic.com
Enter the keywords Gold Rush

GLOSSARY

agricultural (ag-ri-KULCH-uh-rul) having to do with farming

battalion (buh-TAL-yun) a large unit of soldiers

cosmopolitan (koz-muh-POL-ut-un) appealing and refined in a worldly way

entrepreneurs (ahn-truh-pruh-NURZ) people who start businesses and find new ways to make money

flumes (FLOOMZ) chutes for moving water

gristmill (GRIST-mill) a mill for grinding wheat or other grains

hydraulic mining (hye-DRAW-lik MINE-ing) using powerful streams of water to mine for gold

irrigation (ihr-uh-GAY-shuhn) supply dry land with water for farming

legislature (LEJ-iss-lay-chur) the part of government that is responsible for making and changing laws

missions (MISH-uhnz) church settlements used to spread religious beliefs to native people

prospectors (PRAH-spek-turz) people who searched for gold

Puritanism (PYOOR-ut-un-iz-uhm) a religion based on a strict moral code

ratified (RAT-uh-fyed) agreed to or approved officially

sluices (SLOOS-iz) devices used to control water's flow along a path

speculators (SPEK-yuh-lay-turz) people who invest money in an attempt to make a profit

Page numbers in *italics* indicate illustrations.

Act for the Government and Protection of Indians (1850), 50
advertising, 18, 22, *22*
agriculture, *6*, 10, 11, 28, 33, 35, 36, 43, 47, 48, 51
American River, 12, 18, 23, 25, 37
Aspinwall, William Henry, 36, 56
Australia, 15, 35

Brannan, Sam, *16*, 17, 18, 19, 20, 31, 57, *57*

California Star newspaper, 17
California Trail, 22–23
Camp Salvado, 27
Catholicism, 6
Chinese Camp, 27
Chinese miners, 27, 45, *45*
Civil War, 41
claims, 25
Clapp, Louise, 27
Clay, Henry, *40*
Compromise of 1850, 40–41, *40*
constitutional convention, 38–39, 41
construction, 11, 14–15, 26, 28–29, 31, 33, 36
crime, 29, 31, 46, *46*, 50

deaths, 22, 29, 43, 46, 49–50
delegates, 38–39, 41
discovery, 7, 15, 17, 19–21, *20*
diseases, 22, 23, 50

education, 9, 28, 33

fires, 30, 31

First Presbyterian Church (San Francisco), 30
Foreign Miner's Tax, 45

gambling, 29, *30*

Hargraves, E. H., 15
hydraulic mining, 47–48, 47, *48*, 49, *49*

indentured workers, 50

Levi Strauss & Co., 31
long toms, 21, *21*, 47

manufacturing, 35
map, *52–53*
Marshall, James W., 11, 12, *12*, 13, 14, 15, 17
Mason, R. B., 19–20
Matteson, Edward, 47
merchants, 17, 18, 20, 27–28, 36, 39, 55
Mexican-American War, 12, 19, 38, *39*, 57
Mexican workers, 7, 45–46
Mexico, 6, 12, 34
mining towns, 7, 26–27, *26*
missions, 6–7
money. *See* wealth.
Mormons, 11, 12–13, *13*, 14, 17

Native Americans, 6, 7, 10, 22, 23, 49–50
New Helvetia settlement, 10, *10*
New York Herald newspaper, 20

Pacific Mail Steamship Company, 36–37, *36*, *37*
Panama Railroad, 37, *37*
panning, 18, 21, 44, *44*
People v. Hall (1854), 45
Polk, James K., 21
pollution, 47–48, 49
population, 7, 29, 34, 35, 50

railroads, *32*, 33, 36, *36*, 37, *37*
ranches, *6*, 7, 11, 12, 39, 50
religion, 6, 11, 12–13, *13*, 14, 17, 30, 33
Riley, Bennet, 38
roads, 33, 36

saloons, 11, 27, 28
San Francisco, California, 13, 17, 18, *24*, 25, 27, 29, *29*, 30, 31, 34, *34*, 35, *35*, 37, *54*, *55*
San Francisco Pacific News, 13
Sawyer, Lorenzo, 48
settlers, 7, *7*, *8*, 22, 23, *23*, 50
Sherman, William Tecumseh, 19, *19*, 57
slavery, 40–41, *41*, 46, 50
SS *Central America* (steamship), 37, 38, *38*

state constitution, 38–39, 40
statehood, 38, 39–40, *39*
steamships, 36, 37
Strauss, Levi, 31, *31*, 57, *57*
supplies, 12, 18, *18*, 19, 21, 23, 27–28
Sutter, John, *8*, 9, 10–11, 12, 13, 15, 20, 21, 37, 43, 56
Sutter's Fort, 10, *10*, 11, *11*, 12, 17, 43
Sutter's Mill, 11, 12, 13, 14–15, *14*, 19, 43

taxes, 45, 48
tools, 18, *18*, 21, *21*, 28, 47
transportation, 7, 17, 21–23, *22*, *23*, *24*, 25, *32*, 33, 35, *35*, 36–37, *36*, *37*, 38, *38*, 54
Treaty of Guadalupe Hidalgo, 19, 38

U.S. Congress, 21

wealth, 9, 12, 18, 19, 20, 23, 29–30, *30*, 37, 45, *54*, 55
Williams, Albert, 30
women, 27, 28–29, *28*

ABOUT THE AUTHOR

Peter Benoit is a graduate of Skidmore College in Saratoga Springs, New York. His degree is in mathematics. He has been a tutor and educator for many years. Peter has written more than two dozen books for Children's Press. He has written about ecosystems, disasters, and Native Americans, among other topics. He is also the author of more than 2,000 poems.